The Fun Way to Health And Vitality

Shirley Cook—busy homemaker, wife and mother of six children—shows you how to get started in the world's fastest-growing participant sport. DIARY OF A JOGGING HOUSEWIFE will show you:

- How to get started without getting discouraged
- How jogging can help your figure, energy level, heart and lung capacity, and mental attitude
- What to wear, and what *not* to wear
- How to progress slowly and safely
- How to *enjoy yourself* as you jog
  ... And much more!

From the bestselling author of
DIARY OF A FAT HOUSEWIFE
and BUILDING ON THE BACK FORTY

Diary of a JOGGING housewife

Shirley Cook

Illustrated by the Author

ACCENT BOOKS
Denver, Colorado

MEMBER OF
EVANGELICAL CHRISTIAN
PUBLISHERS ASSOCIATION

Second Printing, 1979

ACCENT BOOKS
A division of Accent-B/P Publications, Inc.
12100 W. Sixth Avenue
P.O. Box 15337
Denver, Colorado 80215

Library of Congress Catalog Card Number: 78-72865

ISBN 0-89636-016-4

On Your Mark, Get Set, Go!

If you're tired of sitting on the sidelines watching the world (and your next door neighbor) run by; if you're depressed, discouraged and down in the dumps; and if you're willing to exchange all that for involvement, energy and a new enthusiasm for life—then this book is for you.

Probably the idea of exerting yourself beyond changing TV channels turns you off. It did me. In fact, just watching Bjorn Borg and Jimmy Conners sliding around the clay court on Sunday afternoon TV left me exhausted and calling for Gatorade. No more.

From a FAT housewife to a JOGGING housewife. Can it really be?

I just got home from a three mile run—thirty minutes of constant jogging, and I feel terrific. If I hadn't experienced it for myself, I wouldn't have believed it possible. It didn't happen all at once. I have been building my strength and endurance day by day, week by week, month by month. And so can you.

I've found something that is changing me (and countless others across the country) physically

On Your Mark, Get Set, Go!

and emotionally. Jogging is not only helping the hefty housewife and the bulging businessman, it is also used as therapy for the mentally ill and for heart attack victims. How could such a simple and inexpensive sport as putting one foot in front of the other be so beneficial? And fun?

Well, God made most of us with two feet and the ability to walk and run. (I say if He'd wanted us to play tennis, we'd have been born with a racket attached to our arm.) He also gave us the desire to play, and that's what jogging is. At least, that's how I feel when I tie on my shoes, leave the breakfast dishes in the sink, and trot down the street with the wind in my hair.

I remember a few months ago how I broke out in a cold sweat as my husband tried to pry my hands off the front door and out into the running world. Today, he has a hard time keeping me off the streets. And since I've discovered how good jogging makes me feel, I want to share it with you—so you can feel good, too. We can be jogging partners.

I also want to share Jesus Christ with you because knowing Him makes me (and all who know Him) happy.

Being physically fit is great, but there's more to life than that. God made man in His image (Genesis 1:27) and until that image is formed in man by the new birth (Galatians 4:19) we are incomplete, no matter how much head knowledge or physical strength we have.

It's as simple to enter into God's family as it is to put one foot in front of the other. (If God had wanted us to work our way into Heaven, He wouldn't have sent His Son.)

On your mark. God says we've missed the mark, "For all have sinned, and come short [missed the mark] of the glory of God" (Romans 3:23). So to get on your mark, you come to Jesus Christ, confessing that you are a sinner in need of a Saviour. Romans 10:9,10 says, "That if thou shalt confess with thy mouth the Lord Jesus, and shalt believe in thine heart that God hath raised him from the dead, thou shalt be saved. For with the heart man believeth unto righteousness; and with the mouth confession is made unto salvation."

Get set—to receive Him into your life as Saviour and Lord. "But as many as received him, to them gave he power to become the sons of God" (John 1:12).

Go! As a new creation in Christ (II Corinthians 5:17), get out of that easy chair and get going—TODAY!

1
In A Fixx

Dear Diary

I don't know why my husband can't let sleeping dogs (and wives) lie. Yesterday he brought home *The Complete Book of Running,* by James F. Fixx, and stuck it under my nose.

"Here. Maybe this'll inspire you to get some exercise."

I turned the bright red book over in my hands. The strong muscular legs on the front cover caught my attention. Even the chapter headings sounded interesting, and before I knew what I was doing, I began to read. The more I read, the more I wanted to read.

"Wow, here's all I wanted to know about exercise, but was afraid to ask," I called to my husband in the next room.

Maybe it would be fun to run in the sun, or maybe I'd go after dark so the neighbors wouldn't see me.

As I read that interesting and informative book, I pictured myself whizzing through the park, strong muscular legs lifting my body through the air as deftly

In A Fixx

as the kangaroo crossing the Australian outback. The health benefits alone should have been enough to get me out of my chair—but it was so comfortable to sit relaxed, feet up on a hassock, and read about other people running, that I stayed in that position all day.

I'd almost finished the book by midnight and was so tired thinking about running that I hobbled down the hall and fell into bed.

"Well, honey," my husband whispered, "what do you think?"

"About what?"

"About running. Do you want to start?"

"Oh, yeah, sure."

"How about tomorrow morning?"

"Tomorrow? Isn't that a little soon? Anyway I have a few more chapters to read."

That was the standard answer I gave him. I'd read half a tennis book, three chapters on biking and all but one page of *Caving In*. I was practically an authority on most sports, yet had managed to keep my hands uncalloused, my lungs unwinded and my knees unskinned.

When any of our friends brought up the subject of their favorite sport, I simply opened the appropriate book and spouted words of wisdom. Of course, my words were always second-hand and didn't bear much credibility, but I didn't mind.

Yes, I'd handle running the same way. I would keep turning the pages, but not finish the book.

Dear Partner

I've heard people use my excuse when asked what they think of Jesus Christ as He is revealed in the Bible.

"Oh, I've read the Bible many times," they say, piously looking toward Heaven, "but I've yet to be convinced that Jesus Christ is the only way to God."

Jesus said, "I am the way, the truth, and the life: no man cometh unto the Father, but by me" (John 14:6).

These same friends who have read the Bible dismiss Jesus' words as easily as I do when I read a book that challenges me to get up and move. My muscles may atrophy because of my procrastination; but "the soul that sinneth, it shall die" (Ezekiel 18:4). I hope you aren't hedging about something as important as your eternal life.

Dear Lord

Sometimes when I hear Your voice,
With a shrug and knowing look
I dismiss my duty with the words,
"I know—I've read the Book."

2
Excuses, Excuses

Dear Diary

If anyone has good REASONS for not running, it's me. First of all, I'm over forty (never mind how much) and it is probably too hard on my heart. Of course, when I give blood at the blood bank, they always smile when they take my heart rate and blood pressure. What do they know?

Another thing: I had disk surgery three years ago. All that jogging and jerking would probably put me back in the hospital. How could the doctor be sure I was completely healed?

And how about my weak ankles? I've twisted them so many times simply by stepping off a curb—no telling what would happen while running through the park.

I can't forget how unadept I have been at every sport I've tried. It's downright humiliating. I have a rust-covered ten-speed Gitane bicycle standing against the garage wall because I have an ungrounded fear of derailleurs. I avoid any body of liquid larger than a bathtub because I

Excuses, Excuses

can't even tread water. One day on roller skates undid my spine, and winter sports break me out in red puffy spots. Tennis was also a set of catastrophes, scoring up shin splints and tennis elbow (not to mention a black eye I got from a Wilson No.1).

I'm not surprised that I've done so poorly at sports. It's nothing new. I was always chosen last to be on the sixth grade kickball team. I was third string on the high school volleyball team. I even fell down on my knees just walking across the gym floor to receive the honor of Homecoming princess.

Most people don't realize how unathletic I am. I get a summer tan in the back yard (holding tightly to the chaise lounge), and I keep strong and healthy by mowing the lawn and hanging wallpaper. I'm a spectator, plain and simple. I love "Wide World of Sports," PGA Golf and Wimbledon on the green. I even enjoy watching my children swim, dive, and downhill ski. My husband rides a bike and swings a mean tennis racket, and I'm there cheering. But please don't ask me to participate.

However, running may be MY sport. I don't have to compete. I don't need any special equipment. I don't have to go far away to do it. I don't even have to depend on someone to do it with me. I can start when I want, and stop when I want. Maybe, just maybe I could be a jogger. I'll think about it a little longer.

Dear Partner

Do you have excuses for the things you don't want to do? You may call them reasons, too, but in reality they're excuses. They may even be lies.

God knows our hearts. He says in Jeremiah 17:9, "The heart is deceitful above all things, and desperately wicked: who can know it?"

Let's not offer flimsy "reasons" to avoid doing what's right anymore, whether it is something physical or spiritual. We say we're too tired to attend church, too busy to pray and too preoccupied to read the Bible. We won't witness for Jesus Christ because we don't know how, and we can't give our tithe because we have so many bills.

Do you spell REASON: *E-x-c-u-s-e?*

Dear Lord

As a jockey, I'm too tall
For basketball, too short
No reason why I shouldn't run
And learn to be a good sport.

3
Button Up
Your Overcoat

Dear Diary

As my husband continued to urge me into jogging, I strained for one last excuse. Knowing his interest in the preservation of the environment, I said, "You know, just one more person out there pounding pavement may be the straw that breaks the camel's back."

"What do you mean?" he asked, wrinkling his brow.

"Well, with so many Americans taking up jogging, just think of the vibrations being sent across the earth's crust. My feet may be just the ones to set off a major earthquake that will shake California into the Pacific—never to be seen again." I added that last phrase with special emphasis.

"Oh, come on. Let's go. And put on something warm—it's cold out today."

I dressed in my old jeans, a heavy turtleneck sweater and my leather coat. Then I decided, just to be sure, I'd add

Button Up Your Overcoat

mittens and a knit scarf.

Out I bounded through the front door (after I finally let go of the door jamb) and down the walk, around the corner and *Phew,* I was pooped! At least a half block ahead of me trotted my husband and eleven-year-old daughter. Did you ever watch a young girl run? No effort at all. She just glided along; even came back a few times to help me up off the grass. It was horrible. I hated it. Why did anyone take up jogging? Why not just *talk* about it?

I must be doing something wrong. Didn't the book say I should begin by walking? I had tried to run a race after sitting around for the past ten or twenty years. And I felt so heavy. I may have put on five pounds, but I felt at least thirty pounds overweight. Could I be wearing too many clothes?

When I finally got around the block, I stumbled into the house and kicked off my wedgies. My feet hurt, my ankles wobbled, and my knees and hip joints scraped as I walked.

My husband, cool and relaxed, stared at me. "Why on earth did you wear those shoes? Didn't you read how important it is to wear the right type of shoes?"

"But I don't have any running shoes, and my old 'tennies' have holes in them. What would the neighbors think?"

"Yeah," he said, his eyes wandering over my getup, "what would they think?"

Dear Partner

You can learn from my mistakes, I hope. Don't wear heavy, cumbersome clothes; don't dart out on the first day of jogging like you'd been practicing for the Boston Marathon; and don't wear wedgies—or even your old gardening tennis shoes. There is a right way to begin jogging just as there is a right way to begin walking with Christ.

Don't expect *too* much of yourself as a Christian, either. God is so patient with His children, and gives His Grace to enable us to walk slowly and unencumbered before He prods us along to "run the race."

"He that saith he abideth in him [Christ] ought himself also so to walk, even as he walked" (I John 2:6). Look unto Jesus!

Dear Lord

Weighted down with troubles
I've tried to run ahead
But I'm learning to slow down
And walk with You instead.

4
Goody
Two Shoes

Dear Diary

After reading of the importance of good running shoes in preventing injuries, I headed for my favorite sporting goods store. What a selection. Not only were there a variety of colors, but styles and brands abounded. Which would be the best for me?

I have a problem with shoes anyway. Anything more than a sandal gives me cramps in my toes—a good reason to go barefoot all summer, right? Anyway, I tried on several types, some that were narrow and flat across the toe and some that were stiff and tight around the heel. I finally decided on a broad toe shoe that gave my feet breathing room, yet fit snugly around my heel and arch. Mmmmm, good. Just call me "Goody two shoes."

The first day out in my baby blue Brooks gave me confidence. I felt like a runner—even if all I did was walk. After a week of walking in my jeans, I decided as long as I was going to give this "the old college try" I may as well look the part and invest in a sweat—excuse me, *warm-up*—suit. I was lucky. I found a powder

Goody Two Shoes

blue one on sale for less than the price of the shoes.

I could see why the stress for specially-built shoes. The heel cushioned the jolt normally taken by the knees and back, and my ankles felt stronger than they had in years. My toes didn't even cramp. And with feet that felt good, maybe I had found my sport. At least I'd found a pair of shoes that were comfortable.

The warm-up suit felt good, too, especially on those cool, foggy mornings. As the days grew warmer, though, I decided I needed something cooler. Would I dare be seen in public in shorts? I hadn't even worn them around the house in years—the veins, you know. I convinced myself that it wasn't really "in public" to be seen in the park or neighborhood, especially if I was jogging. It was expected by curious onlookers that a jogger look like one.

I found some shorts that weren't too short. They were made of a knit fabric with elastic around the waist. I bought a big T-shirt to wear with them and as I looked in the mirror I felt good—good about myself and good about what I was doing for myself. There was some sort of psychological lift to tying on my running shoes and stepping into my shorts and T-shirt. I was no longer what I'd always considered myself, a FAT housewife.

Now I was a JOGGING housewife. I had found a sport—my sport!

Dear Partner

It really doesn't matter if you wear a warm-up suit or a pair of knit shorts when you jog, as long as you are comfortable and your clothes aren't rubbing or binding you. It *is* important that you spend a little extra money to get a good pair of shoes. Think how many times your feet hit the pavement in one mile—about 800 times. Then think of the beating your body is taking with each jolt. Don't you deserve the best care for your feet—and body?

God says that as Christian soldiers, we should wear special shoes, too. "And your feet shod with the preparation of the gospel of peace" (Ephesians 6:15). Our feet should be ready to take us to our friends and fellow workers, prepared to share the love and good news with them.

Dear Lord

To go to others
With the Good News
I need to be fit
With gospel shoes!

5
Ah-Ah-Choo!

Dear Diary

After a month of steady progress, walking combined with a little jogging, something disturbing began to happen. I shouldn't have been surprised. It happens every year about this time. As the days grow warmer and little buds poke their green heads out to signal the arrival of spring, I start to sneeze.

It's not the leaves or sprouts of grass or even the daffodils and tulips that drive me crazy; it's those little things that fall off the trees disguised as fuzzy worms. I don't know what they're called, but to hayfever sufferers, they're Public Enemy Number One.

I thought I could ignore them (as they fell at my feet and in my hair) by holding my nose and breathing through my mouth. But the pollen rushed down my throat, too, bringing on wheezes interrupted by "Ker-choos!"

And I had been doing so well—all the way around the park and home in a half hour, about a mile and a half. I'd have to stop running for awhile, hopefully just a couple of weeks, and stay inside with the windows tightly closed and the Allerest nearby.

Two weeks stretched into three and three into five. By the sixth week, I didn't even want to jog. Why should I? It was much easier to stay in with a second cup of coffee instead of running around the neighborhood like a demented fool.

Fool? I would be foolish to give up so

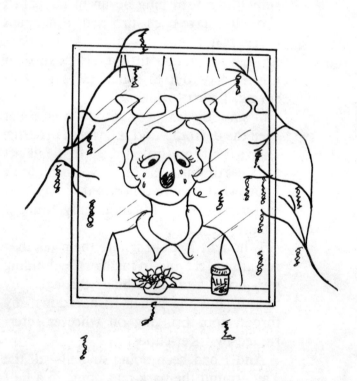

Ah-Ah-Choo

quickly. I had several books by now that convinced me I *needed* to run. I'd never heard the term *cardiovascular* until I began perusing running books. It has to do with the strength and health of the heart and blood vessels. I also learned that "*aerobics: promoting the supply and use of oxygen*" is what contributes to cardiovascular health, and since jogging is an aerobic exercise, it improves the body's ability to take in and deliver oxygen to the body tissues.

So what does all that mean to me? It means more energy, strength and zest for living. It means a stronger heart, sharper mind, and possibly longer life. It means FUN.

There are other aerobic exercises besides walking and running, but since they are rope skipping, running-in-place, bicycling and swimming, they're not for me.

I had to make up my mind all over again to tie on my running shoes, slip into my shorts and T-shirt and step out the front door.

Oh, what a surprise. The first day out, I was winded after walking a block. My mouth was dry and cottony before I had jogged ten steps. I'd lost all I'd gained. I had to start from crawl and build up again.

Next spring, I'll be ready for those fuzzy worms. I plan to visit my allergist early. It's the early bird who gets the worm, you know.

Dear Partner

Sometimes we suffer setbacks in our spiritual lives, too. The common term for it is backsliding, and it happens when we neglect our spiritual exercise—studying the Bible, praying and speaking to others of Jesus. To lay off any one of these for a time weakens our testimony. Let's determine to keep on the move physically and spiritually.

"And herein do I exercise myself, to have always a conscience void of offence toward God, and toward men" (Acts 24:16).

Dear Lord

If I don't walk ahead
I won't stand still
I keep slipping back
And my progress is nil.

6
If At First . . .

Dear Diary

Well, I've begun running again. I guess
you could call it running. I decided to do
it right this time because by now, I knew
from the books I'd read, I had started
wrong the first time. Too hard—too fast.
Most of the books advised seeing a doctor
before beginning any new form of exercise. That's not only a good idea, but it
protects the author in case the reader has
a heart attack the first time out. So I,
too, say, "See your doctor." (Whew, now
I'm safe.)

Seriously, the visit to the doctor should
not be overlooked. Tell him that you want
to begin a progressive jogging program.
He'll let you know if there is anything to
prevent you from doing so.

If you are over 35 or heavily
overweight, sports doctors strongly
recommend a "stress test." This is simply
a careful monitoring of your heart and
lung performance during a brief period of
controlled exercise (such as walking on a
treadmill). Potential problems related to

exercise are much more likely to show up during the stress test than during a normal physical exam.

By far, most people in fair-to-good condition—if they use common sense and start out slowly—should have no problems with a running program. A recent issue of *The Reader's Digest* reports the good benefits running has on lower back pain; and that's about the only medical problem I've had for several years.

When I get up each morning, I'm so stiff and sore that I have to hold onto the sink with one hand while I wash my face with the other. The trip to the kitchen from the bedroom is with the movements of a mechanical robot—unwinding. How could someone with a back like mine jog? I had heard all kinds of "authoritative" advice from well-meaning friends and family. They said I would lose my shape, develop thick ankles, rupture my disk, wear away my hip sockets and get bags under my eyes.

But I would answer, "James Fixx says . . . and Joe Henderson writes . . . and Dr. Sheehan (he's my favorite) says . . ." And with such authorities behind me, I began (slowly) to walk five or ten minutes, then jog five or ten.

It helps me get started sooner each morning (I like to go while the world is still fresh and quiet) if I faithfully do some warm-up exercises. Stretching before your run will help prevent muscle-pulls, and will make the effort so much easier. I don't like to do very many, because I hate exercise, per se, but there are a few that don't seem like exercise and do get my legs and back loosened up before I start moving down the street to the park.

The first is a back stretcher. You bend from the waist, keeping your legs straight and letting your arms and head drop—and just hang loose. You don't bounce or stretch, just hang for about one minute. Do it two or three times.

The second one I like is a calf stretcher, and it feels so good both before and after a run. Stand two or three feet away from the wall, leaning on the wall with your hands. Then, keeping your feet flat on the floor, lean into the wall and hold the stretch for ten seconds. Push away, then repeat. Like slow push-ups, only they're push-aways. Some runners find it even more effective to do this exercise one leg at a time.

My third warm-up stretch is for those important hamstring muscles. Place your right leg up on the back of a chair or on the third or fourth step of a staircase. Then, without jerking, slowly stretch that leg by trying to touch the extended foot with your right hand. Hold the stretch for ten seconds, then repeat the exercise with your left leg.

It's just as important to exercise after running as before, because the muscles tighten up as you run, and if you stop suddenly without "warming down" you can get cramps in your legs or even more serious problems.

Dear Partner

The Boy Scouts picked a good motto: "Be Prepared." It's a good motto for runners and Christians, too. Have your spirit, mind and body prepared before charging out the front door. Be ready to meet the world by first meeting with the Lord. ". . . prepare your hearts unto the Lord and serve him only" (I Samuel 7:3).

Dear Lord

Help me to take time
To be alone with God
And not rush in, where
Angels feared to trod.

7
Hey, Comrade!

Dear Diary

After only a few weeks, my husband decided jogging was not his sport. I don't know if it was too slow, too tedious, or if, as I like to think, I ran him into the ground.

Oh, he started out like a greyhound in pursuit of a rabbit, but after a few blocks, there he was panting and puffing as I plodded slowly by. I guess he never read the story of the hare and the tortoise. I wasn't sure if I'd enjoy running alone (although I was alone anyway with my husband two blocks ahead of me), but I wanted to keep on with the jogging.

So I did. I wasn't with anyone, but I wasn't really alone.

Each day on my way around the park and home, I met walkers and joggers of every description—and I immediately felt a part of some special society of "athletes."

They even recognized me as being one of them with a "Hi, there," a "Good morning," or sometimes just a nod and

slight movement of the lips. There was a
pretty young girl in cute yellow shorts and
a blue scarf tied around her head, a dark
wavy-haired guy with rippling muscles, an
overweight man with a dog on the end of

Hey, Comrade

a rope and several women of various ages and stages of jogging progress.

Each one seemed to light up as we met with a word and nod. I suppose seeing me gave them the same spurt of energy I received from them. There's that unspoken encouragement that says, "You can do it—*I* am." Or, "Just a little farther." One slightly bulging comrade gasped to me in passing, "They *say* it's good for us."

Yes, it is good for us, and that's the camaraderie we feel when we see each other. We know we're doing something for ourselves that, although it takes effort and discipline, will improve us not only physically but mentally. We know the deep breathing that accompanies our jogging strengthens our hearts and sends the blood rushing through every part of our bodies. And we know that when we get home, although we'll be tired, breathless, and sweating, we'll feel more alive than ever before and ready to face a day filled with possibilities.

I've observed the oneness shared by men that drive the same kind of sports car or ride bicycles. I've seen the fraternal spirit as they pass each other with tennis rackets under their arms—and now even I belong to a fraternity, and it's great. I may never meet Dr. Sheehan or Kathryn Lance, but we're members of the same club. We share that exhilaration of pounding feet and heart as we run in the great outdoors.

Dear Partner

There's another society I belong to that's even closer than my new running group. It's the society of believers in Jesus Christ. It's called the church. It's not just a local group of believers, although that has its special place, but it's a fellowship of everyone who has been redeemed by the blood of Jesus Christ. We are members for all eternity. We may not have any of the same interests socially, academically or culturally, but there is a oneness, a bond stronger than any earthly tie.

We share the same LIFE, the life of the Son of God. Only forgiven sinners are eligible for membership. Are you?

"He that hath the Son hath life; and he that hath not the Son of God hath not life" (I John 5:12).

Dear Lord

When I feel lonely
I remember with cheer
I'm alone—but not alone
For Christ is always near.

8
A Time To Run

Dear Diary

John and Ida, a happy working couple, look forward to a long quiet run after a day in the city and an hour battling traffic to the suburbs. Alex spends his lunch hour in running shoes, dodging between shoppers and traffic lights instead of relaxing over a heavy lunch at the corner cafeteria. Dave and Robert wait till dusk to don their running clothes and jog down a country lane. But all have a time to run—a time set aside for themselves, either to unwind or wind up. I prefer the early morning wind-up.

In the beginning, it was hard to dress in jogging clothes before waking my husband for breakfast (let's face it—it was hard to dress in anything; I loved to slouch around in robe and slippers for a couple of hours). To be honest, some mornings I would rather pull covers over my head than a T-shirt, but once I'm ready to go, I feel the tug of a fresh new day on my calves and hamstrings. I don't eat breakfast with my husband anymore, just a glass of orange juice. But he doesn't seem to mind. Since it's better to run on an empty stomach or wait at least two hours after eating to run, I breakfast after my shower.

After warm-ups, I start off by walking—long fast strides—for the first block. Then I begin a slow jog. By now my body

A Time to Run

has awakened enough not to go into shock. I hold my arms parallel to the ground, hands loose and unclenched, and swinging naturally with the movement of my body.

Tense neck muscles loosen up and I concentrate on relaxing my legs and ankle joints. Breathing deeply and slowly, I feel the tempo of the quiet, slowly-awakening world around me. Birds chirp a good morning to their nestlings. A soft breeze rustles leaves overhead. An alarm clock buzzes in a drape-drawn house.

I round the corner and pick up speed. A soft mist rises from the dew-covered grass of our neighborhood park. Two men play tennis. Another is mowing his lawn. Birds tiptoe through the grass, their heads bobbing. A jogger bounces across the street ahead of me and disappears between the trees.

The mower stops. Birds settle down to breakfast. I run. Quiet. Only one sound now. Rubber soles slapping the pavement. Oh, yes, another. Breathing. In—out. I love it. This quietness, this time to run.

Around the park once more and then it's time to start home. There's a daughter to get off to school and a house to clean. There's a committee meeting to attend and a chapter to write. But now I'm ready, ready for the day—because I took time. Time to run.

Dear Partner

We always find time to do what we think is important—what we really want to do. I'm afraid I often don't give the time to God that I should. And maybe that's why—that word, *should*. When we *should* do something, our old nature rebels; but when we *want* to do something, nothing can stop us. How much do I love God? Do I want to spend time with Him? Am I truly interested in learning His desires for me? Have I a longing to know Him better?

I discipline myself to run. I don't always want to, but I've found I'm happier and healthier when I do. I also know I'm happier and healthier spiritually when I spend time alone reading God's Word and talking to Him in prayer. So I set aside a time to worship, too. "To every thing there is a season, and a time to every purpose under the heaven" (Ecclesiastes 3:1).

Dear Lord

A time to work
A time to play
A time to listen
A time to pray.

9
It Takes Two . . .

Dear Diary

In my morning jaunts around the neighborhood, I noticed most of the women jogged in pairs. *That would be fun,* I thought. Now all I needed to do was find someone who would be interested in putting on running clothes before she put on her make-up, and foregoing breakfast for a run around the park.

During a conversation with one of my neighbors, I asked if she'd ever thought about jogging. She hadn't, but she loved to walk, so we decided to get together the next morning.

I enjoyed the walk and talk, and she liked adding a little jogging to her daily outing. Experienced runners advise us to jog at a slow enough pace to carry on a conversation. At that speed, we are training—not straining. The time went so quickly as we talked about our girls, our husbands and our concerns, that each day I looked forward to seeing my partner and sharing our new sport together.

There were a few days that she had to be out of town, and I excused myself from running those days because "I didn't want to progress beyond her." Then I had to go away, and she waited for me to return. By the time we got back together, we were both out of shape, and decided it

It Takes Two . . .

would be better if we only run together once in awhile and stick to our own training program.

This plan has worked out best for us because we each have our separate interests and daily schedules that make it impossible to run together on a consistent basis. Once in awhile we happen to get out at the same time and meet in the park to finish up our run and catch up on the latest in, "What have you been doing with yourself?"

I still see joggers out together and think of the fun it is to run with someone, but for myself, I do best alone. Maybe it's because I was an only child and learned to identify being alone, not with loneliness, but with solitude: Or maybe it's because I've shared my adult life with a husband and six children and need some space to get myself together before starting the day. Whatever the reason, if you see me out running alone, don't think I'm unfriendly or lonely. I'm happy.

Dear Partner

As Christians, we are never alone. Jesus Christ has promised to be with us always, even to the end of the age. Isn't that good to know? Whether jogging, driving the car or scrubbing a kitchen floor, He is there—caring, sharing, loving.

I remember how before I knew Christ as my own personal Saviour and Lord, I was often lonely—even when in a crowd. I felt alone and apart. I've always loved people and had plenty of friends, but there was the feeling that no one understood me. And it's true. No one really understands anyone. We can try, but our understanding is influenced by our own opinions and background. Only God truly understands me. Only God understands you. And He's the only One you can count on to stay with you whatever happens.

His promise in Hebrews 13:5,6 is one of my favorites, ". . . I will never leave thee, nor forsake thee. So that we may boldly say, The Lord is my helper, and I will not fear what man shall do unto me."

Dear Lord

If I must have a Partner
You're the One I choose
To run the race of Life with—
I know I cannot lose!

10
The Back Nine

Dear Diary

Well, here I am in Monterey, at a convention with my husband. We're staying in a beautiful hotel situated on the edge of a golf course. Looking out the window last evening, I thought how lucky I was to get to come to such a place for three days. Then I wondered if I would have the nerve to get out and run alone in a strange place the next morning. I brought along my shoes and warm-up suit so I have no excuse, except for my natural shyness at trying something new.

After my husband had left the room to attend the all-day meetings, I remembered how a couple of years ago, when we were at the same conference, I hadn't known any of the other wives and had spent the days alone in my room reading. I had even felt self-conscious about eating alone in the dining room. Here I was again—in the same situation.

I zipped up my warm-up jacket and tied on my shoes. As I debated with myself about jogging, I noticed a man running along the path across the golf course. Fantastic! Who could ask for anything more? The path wandered over the back nine and disappeared among the trees. Wisps of fog drifted close to the ground and enveloped the stands of coastal cypress. I had to go.

Oh, what a great run. Up hills and down. Around the green and through the

The Back Nine

rough. It was too early for golfers to have reached the back nine and I reveled in the cool dampness that washed the curl out of my hair and clung to my eyelashes. Gray squirrels scampered across the path ahead of me, chittering to each other. Sea gulls dipped and dove, then disappeared into the west.

My half hour was over and I was tired. But tomorrow was another day. And the next day, too. A trip out of town was not an excuse to take a day off from running, but rather an excuse to explore a place I had never been. Who but a golfer would have a reason to travel those green swells of the back nine? A jogger, of course.

I couldn't help but compare my attitudes today with those of past years. I have a new confidence that I didn't before. Was it because I had overcome my aversion to exercise and have been rising each day with the determination to run? I like to think so.

Dear Partner

You may find as you talk to runners that they have the idea that theirs is the only sport. And they're not content to leave you alone. They want you to run, too. Please be patient. It's only because it gives so much pleasure that we want to share it with others.

Christians excited about Jesus Christ talk about Him, too. They may be called "fanatics" when they share the Good News of salvation through faith in Christ; but like any "fan," Christians have something to shout about.

Running may not suit everyone. Tennis may not. Perhaps you are one who will never exert yourself in physical exercise, but I'll tell you this: Jesus Christ is for EVERYONE. Whatever your temperament, whatever your life-style, Jesus is just right for you. Won't you give Him a try? "Come unto me [Jesus], all ye that labour and are heavy laden, and I will give you rest" (Matthew 11:28).

Dear Lord

A day in my hotel room
I thought would be just fine
Instead I put on running shoes
And jogged Your beautiful
  "back nine."

11
Have A Heart

Dear Diary

I had noticed my neighbor, Mrs. Jones, eyeing me each morning as I ran by, so wasn't surprised when she called out to me today.

"Say, neighbor," she said, "I see you've been doing a lot of jogging lately. Think I could do something like that?"

She paused a minute and rubbed out her cigarette with the heel of her shoe. "I guess I'm a little out of shape, but maybe running would help me."

I waited until she had stopped coughing before I answered. "Have you had a physical recently, Mrs. Jones?"

"Oh, no, don't have time for such things."

She bent over to pull a weed out of the grass, then rose, her face red and her breath coming in gasps. "I think if I just start exercising, I'll feel much better. What do you think?"

"I think you should get some exercise, but you should see your doctor first and do what he says."

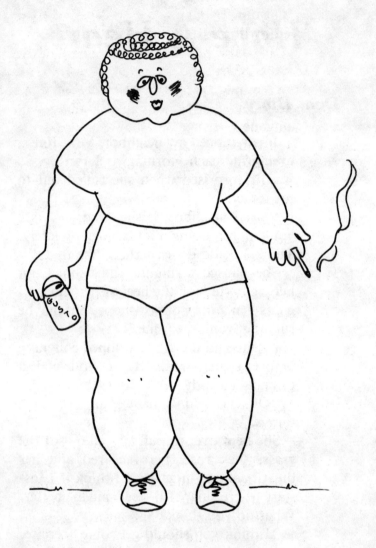

Have A Heart

I don't know what she'll do. I hope she will see her doctor. I hope she loses weight and quits smoking. I hope she begins to enjoy life as she was meant to.

It's said that the persons most likely to have heart attacks are those who are overweight, sedentary and smoking like a chimney. Those individuals, along with anyone over age 35, should take a stress test before beginning a jogging program.

As for those in good health who want to strengthen their hearts and live a longer, healthier life, running may be just the answer. In the few short months I've been jogging, my resting heart rate has already dropped a few beats per minute. That's good. It means that it is doing as much work with less effort. It is stronger and will probably last longer. The increase in oxygen, combined with the contracting muscles in my arms and legs as I run, have been working together to strengthen my heart. Now I'm no expert, but from what I've read, that's the way I understand it.

I've also found that it now takes less time to feel rested after running. I can work longer and harder at other tasks, too. It's not unusual after a morning run to get out and mow the lawns, clean the house and write a few pages of my latest manuscript. I feel good all day and into the evening. I sleep well, too.

Dear Partner

Do you have a heart for running? Don't take unnecessary chances if you are out of shape. But don't make excuses either. I had been sitting around for years, but I started slowly and consistently walking, jogging and occasionally running (not very fast). Take care of that heart. You only get one.

The Bible has much to say about the heart, too. It uses the term to mean *the seat of the affection*. "... Did not our heart burn within us, while he talked with us by the way...?" (Luke 24:32a). How is your heart toward Jesus? Have you allowed Him access to your affections?

Dear Lord

When I read Your Word
And rest at Your feet
My heart grows stronger
With every beat.

12
A Stitch In Time

Dear Diary

When a friend who had been running for several years warned, "Running can keep you in stitches," he didn't mean I'd be laughing all the way home. He meant I could be limping all the way home (and not because of a cut and sutured toe).

Remember when you were a kid and ran races at school? Sometimes you'd get a sharp pain in your side and would have to stop, lean over and breathe deeply before it would go away. Well, that was a "stitch." I can understand how it got its name. It feels just like the doctor is taking one—with a long, sharp needle.

I got my first one after I'd been jogging a few weeks and had decided to pick up my pace. To run faster, I had to breathe faster and gulped in the precious air in short quick swallows. *Ouch.* I just couldn't go on. I bent over, holding my left side (I remember it was my left because of the relief I felt knowing my appendix is on the right). I took several little short breaths, then longer ones, until the

A Stitch in Time

pain had dissipated. When I resumed jogging, it was at a slower pace and with deeper breaths.

When I got home, I flipped through the index in my favorite book on running until I found "Stitch." It was a common malady and one that had a preventative cure. It seems it is caused by incorrect breathing or trapping air in the diaphragm. Learning to breathe with the diaphragm instead of taking short shallow breaths was the answer I was looking for. The author suggested lying on the floor with some books on your stomach; then as you breathe, you watch the books rise, and as the air is exhaled, the books descend. Up—down—up—down. It took a conscious effort as, like many women trying to appear thinner, I had always sucked in the stomach when I inhaled. I had to learn how to breathe.

I tried it the next time I went out for my run: breathe in, stomach out—breathe out, stomach in. It wasn't natural, but my side didn't ache. I'm trying to remember to breathe this way, and I'm sure, in time, it will become as natural as—breathing.

Dear Partner

I've found a way to be freed from the cares that often quench my joy in the Lord. Remember how your physical education teacher said, "Breathe out the bad air, breathe in the good"? One night as I was trying to fall asleep, I felt fearful because of some unsolved crimes that had taken place nearby. Realizing that it was fear that kept me awake, I recalled a verse I had memorized, "Casting all your care upon him [breathe out the bad]; for he careth for you [breathe in the good]" (I Peter 5:7). As I did this deep breathing, I began to relax and was soon asleep, confident that God was in control.

Begin to practice this kind of breathing today, whatever care is troubling you, and you'll find that painful "stitch" disappearing as you trust in God.

Dear Lord

What a pain is worry
What a load is care
All I need is to breathe
In and out—through prayer.

13
Please
Don't Tweeze

Dear Diary

I made a shocking discovery yesterday. It happened as I started into my second mile of continuous jogging. Each day I grow stronger and feel the need for less walking, so I continue to jog past the point of that initial gasping for breath. I was surprised at how good I began to feel after those first ten minutes. That's when I made my discovery.

With the cool morning air rushing past my face I didn't realize little beads of water were forming on my forehead until they had gathered together into one big stream and dripped into my eyes. I was sweating! What would my mother say? She had always told me that horses sweat, men perspire, but girls and women glow. That was more than a glow running down my face. Now I had another decision to make—either buy a headband or let my eyebrows grow thicker.

I didn't know whether I should stop

Please Don't Tweeze

and mop or keep on running. I have to make an embarrassing confession. It felt good. I was exercising hard enough and long enough to work up a sweat. *I must be doing something right,* I thought.

And the surprising thing was, I didn't feel as tired as when I first started out on my morning run. The longer I ran, the better I felt. My legs even seemed stronger as I neared home and eased into a brisk walk.

My husband greeted me at the front door and put his arms around me. "Oh, you're really hot aren't you?" he said, pulling away. "You're all wet."

"I know," I said, wiping the back of my hand across my brow. "I'm finally getting into shape."

And I am. The muscles in my legs are harder now than they've been since I pranced in front of my high school band twirling a baton. My upper arms are tightening from the back and forth movement of the daily run. And everything tingles deliciously after fifteen or twenty minutes of exercise.

I don't mind "sweating" at all, because it does make me "glow." My skin, after a shower, looks alive and healthy. I have more energy for the rest of the day than I dreamed possible. Everything and everyone is more interesting to me now. I may not tell Mother about my sweating;

I'll just let my eyebrows grow—and she'll never know the difference.

Dear Partner

If you're one of those who likes to keep cool and dry, jogging is not for you. Maybe the excessive "glow" is what kept many women from running until recent years. We're learning that it's not unladylike to have strong, active bodies. Men find women even more attractive when they're healthy and involved in doing something good for themselves. And I really care more about others when I feel good. I think we need to be careful about making a "fetish" of exercise, but we have a responsibility before God to keep the body in good shape.

"But I keep under my body, and bring it into subjection: lest that by any means, when I have preached to others, I myself should be a castaway" (I Corinthians 9:27).

We can do that by jogging.

Dear Lord

I'm in a dither
Help me, please
To know if I should
Or should not—tweeze.

14
Dragon Feet

Dear Diary

"Maybe you shouldn't jog today, Mom," my daughter said, supporting me on the way to the front door.

"But I don't want to get out of shape."

"Don't tell anyone, but you LOOK out of shape this morning. What's the matter with you?"

"I don't know," I said, clenching my jaws into a forced smile. "I'm just so tired today—but move out of the way. I'll probably feel better after I've been running a few minutes."

I sort of slid down the front steps and began to drag one foot ahead of the other. *At this rate, I won't even make it to the driveway,* I thought. Maybe she was right. I didn't have winged feet today, just dragon feet. My body—my everything was trying to tell me to take a day of rest.

For an experienced runner, my schedule was nothing. But for an inactive, formerly fat housewife, I'd been pushing myself pretty hard. Out at the break of dawn six days a week had caught up with me.

Dragon Feet

That had always been my problem with anything I started. I went at it too hard in the beginning and then tired before I finished the job. For instance, I don't know how many crash diets I've started and stopped because I became sick of them. I've taken up oil painting with a passion, and washed up before even attempting a masterpiece. I'm the same way about housekeeping. I do great for awhile, then stop completely. Gardening: I have visions of a beautifully landscaped yard and heartily pull and dig up everything until I'm too worn out to replant. I thought being a mother was great too, but after having six babies, I found out I had to keep up the mothering for the next eighteen years. You'd think I'd have learned by now.

Once again, I'd been too enthusiastic and was exhausted.

The experts say that running four times a week is enough to do your heart and lungs good. I could run every other day, or run a couple of days, then take off a couple. The important thing is to listen to your own body. Some people have greater endurance than others, but some days even those people have to sit back and prop up their feet.

I have to keep reminding myself that I'm not doing this (jogging) to compete with anyone or to prove myself to anyone.

I'm doing it because I *want* to.

Dear Partner

A day of rest replenishes your strength and gives you a more objective view of your running progress. In the same way, as Christians, we need a day set aside out of our busy schedules to take stock of our spiritual progress. As we spend time fellowshiping with other believers and worshiping God, we are strengthened for the week ahead.

The Word of God, faithfully administered by our pastors, the music of the redeemed lifted to heaven by our voices and the quiet meditation in the pew all work together to build us up to run the race of Life.

"But they that wait upon the Lord shall renew their strength; they shall mount up with wings as eagles; they shall run, and not be weary; and they shall walk, and not faint" (Isaiah 40:31).

Don't settle for Dragon feet when you can have eagle's wings.

Dear Lord

I thank you for the Lord's Day
When I can stop and rest.
It's also time to separate
The good from what is best.

15
Put Your Little Foot – Right Out

Dear Diary

I have to admit that sometimes I run scared. When I feel this way, my body tenses, my neck muscles constrict and I shuffle. It's all because I have fallen so many times in my lifetime. Suppose I should stub my toe, step in a hole or miss the curb some morning? I can just see myself sprawled in the intersection of a busy street while motorists laugh, point and yell, "Get a CAR!"

I almost stumbled yesterday. I had started my run at a faster pace than usual, so I tired more quickly. By the time I had reached my one-mile-to-home mark, I had a hard time putting one foot in front of the other. My toe dragged across a high spot in the street and threw me forward. Fortunately, I didn't fall, but my nightmare of intersection-sprawl haunted me all the way home.

In the last few weeks, I've been trying to correct several things in my running

*Put Your Little Foot —
Right Out*

style. I'm learning not only from my own mistakes, but from the flaws I see in other runners along my course. Most of the women seem to shuffle on their toes instead of landing on their heels, passing me with a "swoosh-swoosh" sound. I've also noticed that several approaching women throw their feet out to the side instead of lifting them forward. Their bodies twist and turn, using up more energy than necessary.

With the sun at my back, I could see from my shadow that I was doing the same thing. So although I have to concentrate a little more right now on what I'm doing, I think after a while a smooth style will be natural. Besides, lifting my feet higher will make me less likely to trip.

Another thing I'm experimenting with is arm movement. I've had a stiff neck for several days and attributed it to sleeping on a too-big pillow; but now I believe it's caused by the way I hold my arms and body while running.

With my arms held high and close to my sides and my fists clenched, I looked like I was entering a boxing ring. (I could tell by my shadow again.) No wonder the rest of my body was tense and my neck stiff! As I began to relax my arms and hands, immediately I noticed a difference in my neck.

It's also important to keep the head up

rather than bent over like a workhorse pulling a load. A straight body, eyes forward, relaxed arms and hands, and legs and feet that point ahead, combined with deep breathing make for a more enjoyable run—and fewer skinned knees.

Dear Partner

Running should be fun, and not a list of do's and don'ts, but a little foresight can alleviate much correction. How much better to form good habits than have to break bad ones!

The Christian walk isn't through a bed of roses either. (Don't forget the thorns.) I've heard people say, "Christianity is just a religion of do's and don'ts. I can live without it." But can we? Just as we learned, "If you play with matches, you'll get burned," God's Word teaches, "The soul that sinneth, it shall die." We need direction and guidance through life, and we find it in the Bible. "Thy word have I hid in mine heart, that I might not sin against thee" (Psalm 119:11).

Dear Lord

To walk through life is simple
Just put one foot before the other
But I need Your guiding Word
As a child needs its mother.

16
Dodging Danger

Dear Diary

Please tell me I'm not paranoid. I've never been afraid to walk under ladders, play with black cats or spill salt; but since I've started jogging, I find myself ducking shadows, avoiding anything with fur, and dodging cars (even when they're parked). Why all this caution? I don't like pain.

On my morning runs, I've been growled, honked, yelled and chirped at. I'm beginning to wonder if there is a conspiracy abroad to get joggers back into their easy chairs. I had prior warning about dogs. It seems they map out their own territory and anyone crossing that line is in no-dog's-land. Sometimes they bristle their backs; once in awhile they growl and show their teeth; and on their good days, they bristle, bark and bound down the street after you.

Then there's that nice quiet man who lives down the block. Gentle, kind and passive—until he gets behind the wheel of his car. I'm sure he planned to back out of his driveway at just the moment I jogged

Dodging Danger

by. He saw me coming before he got into his car. Then, as I approached him, he gunned his motor, grinned fiendishly and almost knocked the pom-poms off my socks!

According to my running books, I could also expect some jeers from passing motorists. They're usually friendly comments like, "Hey, lady, don't you belong home in your rocking chair?" Or, "I thought molasses in January was slow!" and, "Why don't you just take your Geritol?"

None of these things bothered me, maybe because I had been warned, but yesterday, I had a scare that sent me back to the "book." I found all kinds of dangers listed there, but not one mention of "Blackbirds."

I had been trotting along minding my own business when suddenly a blackbird swooped down squawking and making scary faces. It must have had a nest nearby, but all I could think of was that old nursery rhyme about the four and twenty blackbirds baked in a pie. They not only were a dainty dish to set before the king, they also snipped off the maid's nose while she was hanging out the clothes. (She may have been jogging between the lines.)

It would be an inexpensive "nose job," but like I said, I don't like pain. Tomorrow I'll take a different route to avoid those blackbirds, just like I cross the street when I see a dog ahead and sprint past my neighbor's house *before* he gets into his car.

Dear Partner

It's not paranoid to dodge danger. It's wise. Only the foolish person walks (or jogs) into trouble with his eyes wide open. We can also be alert to the dangers that face us as we walk through life. Satan, the enemy of our souls, has traps set all along the way. He crouches in the shadows, swoops down and runs over us—if we don't watch out. As we read the Word of God, we become aware of his devices and the victory over temptation we have in Christ.

"Be sober, be vigilant; because your adversary the devil, as a roaring lion, walketh about seeking whom he may devour: Whom resist stedfast in the faith . . ." (I Peter 5:8,9a).

Dear Lord

Help me to be wary
Of dangers along the way
By heeding your warnings
And doing what You say.

17
Checkmate

Dear Diary

I just read a newspaper article about a world championship chess match. The part that interested me (I'm not a chess player) was the way one of the champions kept mentally alert. He said that every morning he went on a long run. It not only exercised his body before a day at the chess board, but the greatest benefit he received from his daily run was the sharpening of his mental capacities.

He could practically see the moves that should be made as he puffed his way over hill and dale. He was a winner; not only in chess but in the mastery of his own body and mind.

How does running help the mind? It's probably a combination of things. The aerobic exercise which sends blood and oxygen coursing through every part of the body, including the brain, surely has something to do with the development of mental alertness. And the concentration of putting one foot in front of the other at the beginning of the run, releases the

mind from other thought-cluttering problems. After establishing a comfortable
pace, a runner's mind begins to relax, and
all strength goes into the action of the
body-machine pounding its way mile after
mile.

Some who run ten miles and more tell

Checkmate

of a euphoric state of mind that strengthens and energizes them. Whatever the physical or chemical reason behind it, running does help those who have to think for a living. Corporate executives are running on their lunch hours. Pastors are running in the morning. Secretaries and heart surgeons run in the cool evening hours. And housewives (we think, too) run whenever they can fit it into their busy schedules.

Of course, there's the writer. We sit for hours at a time trying to put interesting words on blank sheets of paper. Sometimes the words don't make any sense, and we have to get away—away from the typewriter, away from the house. What better way to reach out for fresh inspiration than to tie on jogging shoes and run away from those white pieces of paper! And I've often found, when I return home, that I have just the words I had been searching for. My mind and body are—a—a—yes—under control.

Excuse me, I think I'll go out for a run right now!

Dear Partner

It's been said that we shouldn't run away from our problems. True, we must face them. But running around the block may be just what we need to see our problems in the right perspective. Being closed in by our own four walls makes the problem seem bigger than it really is, and when we get outside and see the vastness of the open sky, the strength of the mighty oak and the perfection of the tiny flowers along our paths, we remember God.

". . . it is he that hath made us, and not we ourselves" (Psalm 100:3b). As the ultimate of His creation, we have the power to think and reason intelligently, and we can keep our minds sharp and alert by getting into the game of life today. We won't stagnate if we'll get out of our easy chairs and into the fresh outdoors.

With clear, fresh minds, we can think better about which move to make on our chessboards today and in the years ahead.

Checkmate!

Dear Lord

> *Why should I be a "pawn"*
> *Not knowing where to go*
> *When I can be a "king"*
> *Moving freely to and fro?*

18
Speed Or Spuds

Dear Diary

After running today, I decided I needed to lose ten pounds, so I'm starting on a diet combined with my jogging program. It's not that I'm extremely overweight, although I am five pounds over the 120 I like to be. It's that I can feel that extra five pounds bouncing around with every step I take. In fact, I feel like I'm carrying a ten pound bag of potatoes. I've got more spuds than speed.

I have no aspirations for competitive running, but I know that those who run best are not only thin, they're often gaunt. With fewer pounds to pack around my course, I'll have more endurance, speed and fun.

I don't plan to crash diet. I've learned my lessons well. I'll go back to my well-balanced Weight Watcher menu, and that way I'll be sure of good nutrition. I'm beginning to talk like a "health freak," aren't I?

But since we get just one body in which to live this life, it's important to take as good care of it as possible. We need only look around, and not very far at that, to see how many of our friends and acquaintances are shortening their lives

Speed or Spuds

with overweight. After the age of forty-five, a person only ten pounds overweight increases his chances of early death by eight percent. Think what twenty or thirty pounds will do.

Let's not just think about it—let's do something about it. I've wasted a lot of valuable time thinking when I could have been doing. Thinking about losing weight doesn't do any more good than thinking about running. I know people who think about getting rich, earning a college degree and inventing a better mouse trap. But it's the doers who get ahead—while the thinkers continue to sit and think.

What would you like to accomplish this year? Next year? In your lifetime? Well, don't just sit there. Begin doing it. You may not succeed on the first try, but at least you'll be trying, and each time you'll do better. And one day, you will have accomplished that thing that began as a dream. You will be a doer.

Be in control of your circumstances; don't let your circumstances control you. Life is too short for that.

Dear Partner

Have you ever run around the block carrying a ten pound bag of potatoes? Probably not. Maybe, like me, you've found it tiring just to carry them from the car to the kitchen. So why carry ten, fifteen or twenty pounds of fat on your hips and thighs?

All the books on running tell how easy it is to lose weight by combining diet with exercise. In fact, some even go so far as to report weight loss with just running alone. In the months I've been running, I haven't lost weight—I've been eating QUITE well—but neither have I gained. I have noticed a difference in the 125 pounds I'm carrying, though. It's solid. My body is beginning to be more firm and muscular. So I figure if I do want to lose five or ten pounds, it won't be hard at all as I cut back on the food a little and run a little, too.

What is it that you want to do today? There's real encouragement in the Bible. James 1:22, "But be ye doers of the word, and not hearers only, deceiving your own selves."

Do you want to honor God? Then *do* what He says.

Dear Lord

My legs grow stronger
My pounds grow fewer
When I'm not just a thinker
But also a doer.

19
Beauty
And The Beast

Dear Diary

I've seen Shari at the grocery store looking like a Stepford Wife, at the swimming pool passing as one of Charlie's Angels, and at dinner parties looking as elegant as Princess Grace. And when she asked if she could jog with me today, I hesitated before saying, "Yes."

"Er—ah—I go before seven," I said. "The air is nice and cool then, and the streets almost empty. No one will see you, so don't dress up."

"Oh, that's fine. I'll be ready."

I know it was a dirty trick, but I couldn't wait till seven to see her without make-up. (Was she as pale, dry and wrinkled as the rest of us?) I jogged up to her front door fifteen minutes early.

As she stepped outside, I was sure I heard strains of, "Here she is—Miss America," drifting from the recesses of her already bright and shiny house.

Every hair was in place. Even her make-up was in the right places. Her jogging outfit was color-coordinated and she smelled good!

Probably can't run a block. I'll run her into the ground, I thought. I started jogging, a longer stride than usual, and was surprised to see her keep up with me. She couldn't last much longer at that pace.

Beauty and The Beast

(Could I?) But she did, and talked comfortably as she ran. She told me how much she liked California, and how friendly the people were. She said she often felt lonely, but realized the women in the neighborhood were busy with their families. She hoped that now we would become friends.

Shari was really nice. And I had thought she was snobbish—just because she was so attractive. (I had been the snobbish one.)

As we continued our jogging, I couldn't take my eyes off her. Her hair *stayed* in place. Her clothes didn't sag. She was pleasant to talk to—and she didn't even perspire! I wanted to cross the street every time we met oncoming joggers—I felt like "Beauty and the Beast," with me playing the role of you-know-who.

Dear Partner

I'm sure I have a new friend, one who may one day want to hear what Jesus Christ has done for her.

I think sometimes we are shy or reluctant to share Christ with the "beautiful people." They seem self-sufficient and completely in control of their lives. But no one, however he appears outwardly, is entirely satisfied without a personal relationship with the God who made him. In fact, someone you know may be trying to cover up loneliness and fear with a mask of confidence.

I don't know what Shari's needs are. She seems quite happy; but I do know Christ loves her and died for her sins, and she can be even happier—and assured of eternal life. Let's look for opportunities to speak to others about Christ. Perhaps you'll meet that person as you jog around the block. Or maybe it's that new mother in the PTA, or the newly widowed woman down the street. Whoever it is, wherever you meet, be willing to share Christ's love.

"But sanctify the Lord God in your hearts: and be ready always to give an answer to every man that asketh you a reason of the hope that is in you with meekness and fear" (I Peter 3:15).

Dear Lord

Please change my heart of envy
To one that loves and cares
A heart that reaches out
And gives—and shares.

20
Present Arms

Dear Diary

Only a few short months ago when I looked at my legs in the full-length mirror, I saw two pillars of drooping flab. When I touched my calves, they sunk in.

What a difference! This morning after I returned from my run and had begun my "warm-down" stretching exercises, I looked in amazement at my legs. Were they really mine? They didn't sag anymore. In fact, my calves were hard as rocks, and even my thighs were beginning to harden up. I didn't think my varicose veins showed as much either. I hadn't twisted my ankles or fallen on my face for weeks, so my ankles must be getting stronger, too.

Oh, I could never be an advertisement for Hanes, but I was pleased with the progress I was making.

Later, when I was curling my hair, I noticed that the backs of my arms were tightening up, too. They didn't look like elephant's knees anymore. I had known my legs would lose their fat, but I was

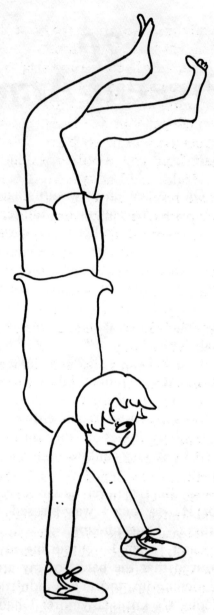

Present Arms

really surprised to see the good effect running has had on my arms.

No, I hadn't been running around the block on my hands. It was from pumping my arms in rhythm with my legs. That swinging motion was firming up the entire upper portion of my body. What a lot to gain from such a little investment!

Health and beauty spas offer much the same results, but at a cost far exceeding the price of good running shoes. And the time spent using exercise equipment after driving several miles is greater than the time spent running each day. Besides all that, I think once a person is "hooked" on jogging, he will continue to practice what he's learned and never return to that old flabby body.

Boy, if I can see such a change after so short a time, how will I look when I'm sixty or seventy years old?

I met an "old" woman with a German accent this morning as I ran through the park. We spoke, and she wanted to talk a minute, so I stopped. She said she walked seven or eight miles every day, summer and winter, and looked forward to many more years of the same. She had a healthy glow on her face and her eyes twinkled as she said, "Better get on there, young one (who, me?), and I'll get on, too."

I've been thinking about her all day. Her arms and legs were youthful looking and she moved smoothly and quickly with a slim, ageless body—and I feel hope.

Dear Partner

Getting out on the sidewalk in jogging clothes may not be as glamorous as an hour or two in a beauty spa. It's more like going to the battlefield than a garden party. Sometimes it's hard—really hard—to run out the front door, but it's worth it. So be a good soldier; slip into your T-shirt, shorts and jogging shoes and present arms—and legs.

Perhaps you face another kind of battle today: a life-changing decision, a painful confrontation, a soul-damaging temptation. There is an answer:

"Wherefore take unto you the whole armour of God, that ye may be able to withstand in the evil day, and having done all, to stand" (Ephesians 6:13).

Dear Lord

Thank you for the armor
Provided for this life
To make a FIT soldier
From a FAT housewife.

21
That Extra Mile

Dear Diary

I did it!

The author of one of my running books suggests pushing harder at least one day a week. He says it would be a good idea to try to double the running time that day, then the next day rest. Well, since Sunday is MY day of rest anyway, I decided to try it today (Saturday). Last night I drove the car around my prospective course and measured it in miles on the odometer. *Four and 8/10 miles!* Could I make it?

I thought about it all evening, picturing myself running around the lake *again,* knowing how tired I usually am after only one trip. But I knew I could stop if I got too tired and walk home. No one was forcing me to do it. I fell asleep dreaming about what an accomplishment that would be for me.

This morning, awaking before my husband, I slipped into shorts, and T-shirt and shoes, did my warm-ups, and started out with one thought in mind. I *can* go that extra mile—or two. There was less traffic than usual—people sleep in on a Saturday morning. The air was fresh and cool (not like yesterday's high of 100°) and I felt good. I began as usual, by walking the first

That Extra Mile

block, then I broke into a slow, steady jog.

The one mile mark. I was breathless but beginning to get my second wind. On I went. Past the marina. Past the apartments and the vacant lot. Then I was running through the neighborhood of new homes with their newly planted lawns and shrubs. The palm trees in the distance told me I was approaching the two-mile mark. Now I was perspiring, but breathing more easily.

I slowed to a brisk walk for about five minutes. I could hardly believe how quickly my strength returned. Rejuvenated and ready to start around the course again, I picked up my pace. A man I'd met my first time around smiled as he ran by. Did he look impressed? I thought so.

I don't know what happened to the next two miles. I was hardly conscious of running. I could hear myself breathing, and occasionally I reached up to wipe the perspiration from my forehead, but the time passed quickly. Without my realizing it, I was soon on my way home.

When I walked (or did I float) in the front door, my husband was as proud of me as I was.

I did it! Only a few months in running shoes and I had jogged five miles. So what if it did take me almost an hour? I enjoyed it and my whole day has been filled with energy and enthusiasm—because I went that extra mile.

Dear Partner

Jesus said in Matthew 5:41, "And whosoever shall compel thee to go a mile, go with him twain." How often we complain when asked to do something that doesn't appeal to us! How we hate to give up our precious time and plans to meet the needs of others. The ideal Jesus was trying to get across is that we should willingly give of ourselves; not just do what is expected, but to go on beyond that and bring unexpected happiness into the lives of friends and family.

How can we do that? By projecting a course and then deliberately setting out to attain it. We can be sure of the Lord's blessing and new energy and endurance in our Christian walk. "Bear ye one another's burdens, and so fulfil the law of Christ" (Galatians 6:2).

Dear Lord

By going that extra mile
We'll be surprised to find
We have new strength and energy
In body, spirit and mind.

22
Don't Cancel My Subscription

Dear Diary

I had never thought of myself as a proponent of the women's movement, but maybe, in a way, I am. It isn't that I have thrown out my ideas of "A woman's place is in the home," because I still love my home. It's that I have been developing a few new ideas: "A woman's place isn't *only* in the home."

What made me realize the change in my interests? It was my daughter, looking through my magazine rack.

"Mom, where's your copy of *Good Housekeeping*?"

"Oh, it must be there someplace."

"No. In fact, I can't find any women's magazines."

"Really?" I said, sliding down on the floor beside her.

It was true. Beautiful women in ruffled aprons arranging pillows on fluffy beds had been replaced by lean (also beautiful) women in tank tops, shorts and jogging shoes. *Runner's World* had crowded out *Good Housekeeping*—not only in my magazine rack, but also in my priorities. It's not that I neglect my home or family, it's just that cross-stitching a tablecloth has lost some of its appeal.

I'm sure that on those cold, rainy days ahead, I'll pick up that tablecloth again. Who knows, I may even finish it some

Don't Cancel My Subscription

year. But right now while the weather is good, my heart is outside—and so is my body. And since my reading material reflects my interests, Bob Anderson's magazine rates high in my "favorite magazine" poll. In it I find articles about health and nutrition and ways to improve my new-found sport.

My husband not only got me started jogging—he was the one who introduced magazines and books about running to me. So I figure he has no complaint if his dinner is late or if I happen to be running around the block when he comes into the kitchen for breakfast. He can yell. He can pout. He can take away my allowance—but may he never "cancel my subscription"!

Dear Partner

Have you taken a look at your magazine rack and bookshelves lately? An inventory may be in order. You can learn much about yourself that may surprise you. (Others may be surprised, too.)

A loved one recently passed away, and as we went through his things we found that he was exactly what he seemed to be. His books (well read) included the classics, poetry and inspirational. We were thrilled to find many Bible study books and devotionals. However, we would have been surprised and deeply hurt if we had discovered books that feed the lower nature instead. Surprised, because he exemplified a follower of Christ—and hurt, because we looked to him with respect and honor.

If you or I should be called away from this life today, how would our friends and loved ones be affected by the reading material they would find in our homes?

Let's do a little housecleaning today. Remember that old proverb, that we are what we read.

"Thy words were found, and I did eat them; and thy word was unto me the joy and rejoicing of mine heart: for I am called by thy name, O Lord God of hosts" (Jeremiah 15:16).

"Till I come, give attendance to reading, to exhortation, to doctrine" (I Timothy 4:13).

Dear Lord

*I should be very careful
Of the books I choose to read
Some encourage giving
While others foster greed.*

23
Ho-Hum

Dear Diary

Down the street—past the white house
—cross the street—to the brick house
—turn the corner—over to the park. Past
the tennis courts and baseball diamond
—cross the street and around the lake—
past the marina, the swimming pool,
the apartments and on the way home.
Ho-hum . . .

Day after day, week after week, month
after month, it was the same. I was getting
bored with my course. It had become
tedious. I could run it blindfolded! I knew
just when I would start to perspire. I knew
how many blocks I had left to go.

Surely after only a few months of jogging, I wasn't ready to give up out of
boredom. I needed to change my
route—at least add some variety to my
daily runs.

So I decided to jog in a different direction. I would run down to the shopping
center and back a couple of days each
week. It felt strange at first. I saw people
and places that were unfamiliar to me.

Ho-Hum

They eyed me suspiciously but soon accepted me as part of the environment. I was no longer bored.

It's so easy to get into a rut, and as runners we need to guard against it. I realize that in some areas there are limited places to run, but you can add variety by running in the opposite direction, or at a different time of day. Try running with a partner instead of alone, or alone instead of with a partner. Do whatever you need to do to keep up your interest and enthusiasm. Boredom can drain away all the fun from running and when it becomes a duty or drudgery, the temptation is to forget it and find something new.

I don't ever want to get bored with running. I enjoy it too much. I like the way it makes me feel—alive and excited about life. So as long as I am able, I'll run—searching out new paths and partners instead of giving in to boredom.

Let's see, tomorrow I think I'll take that road that runs along the levee. It has some hills that will be a challenge and . . .

Dear Partner

So much of our time is spent doing routine tasks. We rise each morning, shower and brush our teeth. We sit down at the breakfast table and eat the same bacon and eggs. We go to work—or stay at home and clean the same house. Day after day, we go our way repeating the jobs we did yesterday and the day before and the day before and . . .

I've found a way to keep a freshness of spirit in spite of routine tasks. ". . . whatsoever ye do in word or deed, do all in the name of the Lord Jesus . . ." (Colossians 3:17).

Whether we are at work, at home or out running through the park, Christ can make a difference. He *is* the difference between routine and inspiration. He is always present; and how can a person be bored in the presence of the Son of God?

He adds sparkle and enthusiasm to life. Let's seek Him out today through the Word of God, then take time to acknowledge Him in the quiet place—and in the everyday activities in which we find ourselves. We'll never be bored again.

"Seek ye the Lord while he may be found, call ye upon him while he is near" (Isaiah 55:6).

Dear Lord

Many folks "drop out"
Because they are bored
But they'd find life exciting
If they would seek the Lord.

24
And For
Accessories . . .

Dear Diary

I always love looking at the last pages in magazines; you can find the most interesting items for sale. The "home" tabloids offer such things as self-watering flower pots, barefoot galoshes and uncurling irons for people with naturally curly hair.

My new "running" magazines had some special offers, too, that assured the buyers of stronger legs, drier foreheads and better times. How could I let another day go by without ordering such surefire accessories?

My mail-order purchases have been arriving steadily for the past few weeks and I have been reading directions and faithfully wearing each and every item—but running isn't as much fun as it used to be.

It takes so long to strap, buckle and snap on all my accessories that I'm tired before I step out the front door. I can't decide which one to leave at home in its box. They are all equally important.

Take my calorie meter, for instance. It tells how many calories I burn up on my daily run. ("Let's see, if I use 300 by running, I could eat that piece of chocolate

And For Accessories . . .

cake for dinner.) Then there's the pedometer. It measures how many miles I run, and that's important, too, isn't it? And of course, no runner should be without a runner's pouch. It attaches easily to my waistband and is convenient for carrying my keys, wallet, and checkbook.

A canteen hooks on the waistband, too. I fill it with water, Gatorade or coffee—whatever I think I'd enjoy on my half hour run. The wrist radio is a must—after all, the morning news is on at 7 A.M., and I wouldn't want to miss it.

I felt I should improve as a runner with so many important accessories, but I'm beginning to wonder if I didn't enjoy my runs *more* when I ran unencumbered. Actually, the only additional equipment other than shoes and clothing that's really necessary is some form of identification—which doctors strongly recommend, just in case something should happen to you while you're running.

Yes, the accessories are nice, but I just may begin to simplify things again. As I jogged yesterday, I saw a man run by (was he ever running) without any accessories. In fact, all he wore was running shorts and shoes. He wasn't even wearing hair—he had shaved it off! Now I've seen swimmers with shaved heads and heard that it helped them swim faster, but a runner with a bald head was something new.

Maybe . . . oh, I don't think my husband would approve of that.

Dear Partner

We can ruin the enjoyment of simplicity by adding unnecessary accessories to our running gear. To run, you need only shoes, comfortable clothes, identification, and discipline.

The same is true in our daily walk as Christians. We can become bogged down with extras: *too many* jobs in the church, trying *so hard* to live the Christian life, and *pushing* our faith at every available opportunity. We are to serve the Lord, obey the Word and witness to the lost, but when it becomes a burden rather than an expression, we have complicated our relationship to Christ. Walking with Him, we need only faith, love and obedience; anything more is an unnecessary accessory.

". . . let us lay aside every weight . . . and let us run with patience . . ." (Hebrews 12:1).

Dear Lord

The way to Heaven
Is by faith ALONE
All my works can't
For sin atone.

25
Rah-Rah-Rah

Dear Diary

Last night while attending a dinner party, I couldn't keep my mind on the conversation directed toward me, because I could overhear my husband talking to the man across the table.

"Oh, you should see my wife run. Every morning, as faithful as clockwork, she gets out and runs three miles!"

I glanced in his direction. Was that pride on his face for *me*? I turned my attention back to the woman next to me, but was aware of the words of praise my husband continued to bore his listeners with. Wow! What a guy.

I love to run, but I love my husband even more, of course, and wouldn't even consider getting out to jog every morning if he objected. But he has consistently encouraged me—and I love him for it.

My children make up the rest of the cheering section. I'm sure they've always thought of me as "Dear old Mom," but they seem to light up whenever the subject of jogging comes up.

"How far are you running now, Mom?"

"You like your Brooks? I've got Nikes."

"Hey, isn't our Mom something else?" All these words from my children keep

Rah-Rah-Rah

me going. I guess the years of encouraging them in their pursuits are coming back to me a hundredfold.

My neighbor's husband is proud of her, too. She says he is at the door waiting with a towel in his hand when she comes in from her run. He's even willing to fix the children's breakfast while she is out jogging. We're fortunate to have husbands like that. Some women must give all their time and attention to their husbands and home; I think a man who requires everything—every waking minute of his wife's time—is insecure and lacks confidence in himself. A man sure of his position in the family gives his wife the freedom to be herself.

This freedom works both ways, though. I try to give my husband breathing room, too. I don't require his constant attention. I know he loves me—and he knows I love him—even though our interests may take us in different directions.

Dear Partner

The author of one of my running books says that if your husband ridicules or scoffs at your interest in running, you'll probably end up a non-runner or a divorcee. I hope you don't have to make that choice. Sometimes a little compromise can be worked out, and you'll both be happy. If he likes you to be at the breakfast table, jog after he leaves for work. If he objects to your running around the block in shorts, wear a warm-up suit.

As Christian wives, our first obligation is to our husbands. We are to honor and respect them; and put their desires before our own. Our children also deserve our time and interest—let's give it to them. As we fit into God's perfect plan, He will bless us with families that love and respect us, too. We may even overhear them say, "Our Mom is a jogger; she bakes good cookies, too."

"Her children arise up, and call her blessed; her husband also, and he praiseth her" (Proverbs 31:28).

Dear Lord

Thank you for a family
Who gives me their support.
They even offer praise
As I pursue my "sport."

26
Jogger "Junkie"

Dear Diary

I think the federal government should insist that all running shoes be labeled, "Caution—May Be Habit Forming." I didn't know what my friend Ron meant when he told me I would become addicted to running. Those words were spoken shortly after I began my jogging program.

"Addicted? How could anyone be addicted to jogging?"

"Just you wait and see," he said. "It gets in your blood. You'll be miserable if you have to stop for any length of time."

That was the most ridiculous thing I had ever heard. I'd been jogging for about two weeks, and I would gladly have given it up—at that time.

Now, after only a few months, I find I'm already a "junkie." I have withdrawal pains if I have to forego jogging for more than two days.

I discovered my "addiction" last week when I had to go out of town. It would have been improper, under the circumstances, to take along running shoes

Jogger Junkie

and jog before breakfast, so I left them at home.

The first morning wasn't too bad; I was accustomed to resting one day a week anyway. The second day, my breathing was slightly erratic, but I managed to quell my anxiety with a second cup of coffee. The third, fourth and fifth days were agony—sheer agony. My legs twitched, my fists flexed and I found myself more than once running in place at inopportune times. Was I ever glad to get home. I didn't even wait until morning, but put on my shoes and took off for the park before dinner.

Ah—that's better.

I don't understand why jogging is habit forming. Maybe it's the deep breathing, and the bloodstream is crying out for all that good oxygen it's recently been getting. Whether it's a physical or a psychological reaction, I don't know; but I do know this—it's a good habit and one that doesn't need to be broken, but continued for good health.

Next time I go out of town, I'll pack my running shoes right along with my toothbrush.

Dear Partner

I've found it's usually easier to acquire a bad habit than a good one. However, the habit-forming process of running, though not easy, has been a pleasure. Sometimes while running I think *Why am I doing this? I'm so tired. It's so hard.* Then when I get home, I feel so exhilarated that I want to go right out again!

A "Quiet Time" with God each morning is a habit that needs attention, too. It's often hard to get up a little earlier to spend time alone with the Lord. I've found myself thinking, *If only I were still in bed.* Then as we form the habit, if a day goes by without spending time in the Word and prayer, we feel empty and frustrated. We need that spiritual exercise and deep breathing of the presence of God. We are "addicted" to fellowship with the Lord of the Universe—and it's good.

"O God, thou art my God; early will I seek thee: my soul thirsteth for thee, my flesh longeth for thee in a dry and thirsty land, where no water is" (Psalm 63:1).

Dear Lord

Habits can be good
Habits can be bad
Spending time with You
Is the BEST I've ever had.

27
Stinging
In The Rain

Dear Diary

The first rain of the season. I heard it during the night, coming down hard and steady. I'd never run in the rain before and was looking forward to it (sort of). Should I wear galoshes and carry an umbrella?

With the shorter days of winter, ·I'd been running after breakfast when everyone had gone to work and school. But the dark clouds still hung ominously overhead, blocking out the sunlight, and I was tempted to stay inside.

Oh, come on. The first time is always the hardest.

After my warm-up routine, I dressed in my nylon warm-up suit. Although it was cold outside, I knew after a few minutes of jogging, I'd be warm, so I didn't want to overdress with extra sweaters. Besides, absorbent clothing would soak up the rain and be heavy. I tied a scarf around my head to keep the wet hair out of my eyes

Stinging in the Rain

and slowly ventured out the front door.

The rain fell softly and steadily like my morning shower, so in I plunged. "Slap—slap" (or was it "slop—slop"?) went my feet on the wet sidewalk. The cool drops splashed against my face like stinging nettles, dripping off my nose and chin. It was uncomfortable at first, but after a few minutes, I began to enjoy my first "Rain Run."

Everything was so clean and fresh. The sidewalk ahead shimmered and the leaves on the trees sparkled like jewels. I met several joggers who looked like drowned rats with smiles on their faces. On I ran, splashing through puddles, the rain soaking through my clothes and spattering my pants with droplets of mud.

Such freedom! My wet clothes and stringy hair were of no concern. My face didn't sting anymore; it just felt cold, and wet and a little numb. I was a child again, running—playing—splashing—singing in the rain.

Dear Partner

There will be many days throughout the winter months when it is raining or snowing violently and running would not only be foolish, but impossible. Days like that we'll have to get out the jump rope. But most days we can learn to cope. We'll just have to use our imaginations and common sense.

Our days aren't always sunny. Often dark clouds obscure our vision of God and we feel alone and frightened. He has promised strength for those dark days and we can experience that strength as we step out by faith in the Word of God. The trials and temptations that come our way may discourage us, and we may feel like hiding our heads under a blanket, but remember that just as the sun is still shining behind those dark winter clouds, God is still reigning no matter what storms are forecast.

It's such a comfort to know that any testing that comes our way has been permitted by God in His all-knowing wisdom and love. And because He has permitted it, He will also give us the grace to brave it—and come out the victors. So don't be afraid to get your feet wet, for "The eyes of the Lord are upon the righteous, and his ears are open unto their cry" (Psalm 34:15).

Dear Lord

Though the day is dark and dreary
I have no need to fear
I can face my trial with confidence
For God is always near.

28
Over Hill,
Over Dale

Dear Diary

As I steadily progressed in my jogging program, I felt the need for more stress. My entire course is on flat ground and I have had no experience running on hills.

Everything I'd read about them scared me. It all sounded so painful. There's that terrible hill at the end of the Boston Marathon that about finishes off anyone who has survived to that point. There are races that take place on Pike's Peak and several other mountains throughout the country.

Well, there are no mountains near me, or even hills for that matter, but I did notice a steep incline up to the Marina that I thought would give me some "hill" stress.

"Over hill, over dale, I will hit the dusty trail . . ." I planned, this morning, to finish my jogging at the marina. I've found that I feel better at the end of my run than at the beginning, so by the time I reached the hill, I thought I should be breathing easily and my muscles would be warmed up. Oh, how glad I am for that

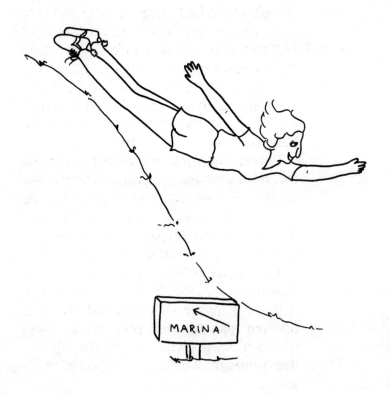

MARINA

Over Hill—Over Dale

"second wind." It usually comes after I've been running for about ten minutes, but then I feel it again after twenty minutes (a third wind?) and at that point I'm sure I could run another hour.

I started at a moderately slow pace to save my energy for the hill, and by the time I reached it, I knew it would be easy. And it was. I had to lean a little and land more on my toes than I had been used to, but up I went with little effort, then along the waterfront and down the other side, back to my usual route. I really enjoyed the run downhill. I felt that if I stretched out my arms, I would glide down it like a huge bird.

I think tomorrow, I'll run up and down the hill twice, then increase it every few days, so I can really get the feel of hill running. The exercise will be good for my thighs, too. So far, most of my muscle development has been in the calves.

I'm certain I'll never run the Boston Marathon or Pike's Peak, but I can dream I'm conquering those hills as I lean into my hill and climb up to the marina.

Dear Partner

Are you afraid to try new things? I think we sometimes hold back for fear of failing more than the possibility of pain. What hills do you see ahead in your life?

Is there an unfulfilled dream that looks too high and hard to climb? How will you ever know if you don't try? Maybe you will fail the first time, but there are some lessons to learn along the way that will help the next time you start up that hill. And one day, if you persevere, you will not only reach the top—you will have become a stronger, more fulfilled person than you thought possible.

Stepping out in faith is much like running uphill. We don't learn to run on hills by continually running on flat terrain; and we don't learn to trust God by always "playing it safe." Let's be willing to suffer a little discomfort if it means a stronger body—and spirit.

"I will lift up mine eyes unto the hills, from whence cometh my help. My help cometh from the Lord, which made heaven and earth. The Lord shall preserve thy going out and thy coming in from this time forth, and even for evermore" (Psalm 121:1,2,8).

Dear Lord

> To climb the hill of faith
> I need to take Your hand
> You'll lead me to the top
> And give me strength to stand.

29
Strains, Sprains And Pains

Dear Diary

Oh, it hurts—here!

I haven't had any injuries since I started jogging. That is, until yesterday. As a beginner, I couldn't go fast enough to hurt myself, and besides that, I'm extraordinarily cautious about lumps, bumps and holes.

I almost got it the other day, though. I was only a block from home and had picked up my speed a little. Familiar with the area, I was looking this way and that, enjoying the scenery, when I (just happened?) to look down in time to lengthen my stride and avoid landing on a beer bottle! I hate to think what could have happened if I hadn't seen it.

Yesterday's injury wasn't caused by falling, but by trying to race with myself. I wanted to see how fast I could run. When I reached the park, I decided to race all the way down the paths, then slow to a jog the rest of the way home. Instead,

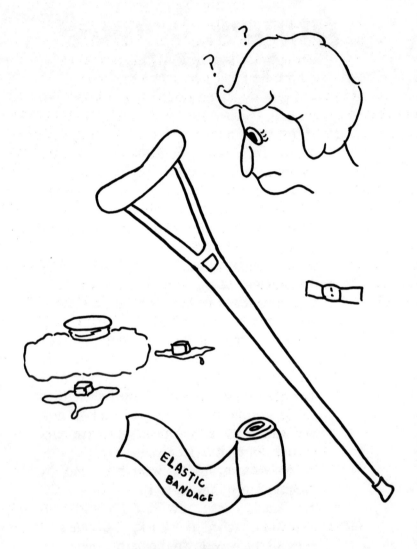

Strains, Sprains and Pains

I ran halfway through the park and limped the rest of the way.

When I felt that sharp pain in my knee, I looked quickly around to see if someone lurking behind a bush had thrown a dagger at me. Oh, it hurt. By the time I reached the house, I had a swollen knee.

I put my leg up on the hassock with an ice bag, reached for Fixx's book and turned to the chapter on injuries. I was relieved to read that I wouldn't have to stop running, but could cut down on the mileage for a few days. I was even more relieved to find that my injury was a common one. (If it isn't better in a few days, I'll try to find a doctor who also runs, and let him treat it.)

Evidently most injuries occur to those who have been running awhile and either push themselves too hard, or after a long workout, injure themselves when they are tired. I thought I would be satisfied to jog three miles a day for the rest of my life; but the three miles is no longer the challenge that it was. I want to better my endurance by either running longer or harder. Since it's the aerobic exercise I'm interested in, I'll probably choose "longer."

Dear Partner

Do you have any strains, sprains or

pains? If so, be sure to treat them properly. Don't ignore them and hope they'll just go away. You may need an ice pack, an Ace bandage or inserts for your shoes. Whatever it is, take care of yourself, so you can be sure of many more miles of running fun.

Sometimes we need to go to a professional for a correct diagnosis; we can't treat our own injuries. In the same way, there are times when we are hurting inside and don't know what to do. God knows. He made us and has the perfect treatment for every pain.

My natural reaction when hurt by an unkind or thoughtless remark is to snap back and inflict pain, too. But that isn't God's way. Think how Jesus responded to those who nailed Him to the cross. "Father, forgive them; for they know not what they do . . ." (Luke 23:34a).

Jesus is the answer to all our questions. As we look at His life, we find the perfect cure for every pain.

Dear Lord

> *My desire is*
> *To see Your face*
> *So I press on*
> *To win the race.*

30
Keep On Trackin'

Dear Diary

This may be the last chapter of this particular book, but it's only the beginning of a new chapter in my life. I've been jogging long enough to know that I thoroughly enjoy it—and will continue to enjoy it, hopefully, for the rest of my life. I'm not running daily to lose weight (though I am losing) and my primary reason to keep on jogging isn't even for the health benefits I'm realizing daily. I intend to "Keep on Trackin' " because it's fun and I like to do it.

Maybe that's not a very good reason for doing something, but it's a more lasting reason than "duty." I hope I improve noticeably in my time and distance in the years ahead, but if I don't, it won't bother me, because I'm not competing or trying to impress anyone.

Dear Partner

What are your goals for your running future? Are you content to jog thirty minutes a day at least four times a week for fitness, or have you aspirations to enter some races? More and more races are opening up in practically every city. Distances vary, and everyone from begin-

Keep on Trackin'

ning jogger to world-class marathoner is welcome to participate.

Whatever your goals are, keep working toward them. Don't give up when you feel tired and have Dragon feet, and don't allow flimsy excuses to keep you from trying out a new sport.

I hope I've been able to encourage you to get out and run for your life. Maybe my experiences as a jogging housewife will be the inspiration you need to get out of your easy chair and run around the block. You won't be alone. Thousands are tying on running shoes every day and heading for the great outdoors. (The popularity of jogging should be evidence of the enjoyment in it.)

Just as there are always new horizons to conquer in the physical realm, there are exciting adventures ahead for those who know Jesus Christ as personal Saviour. I've read some articles written by runners who say they've found a religion in running. They speak of being "born again" through the new physical life they have found in the discipline of long distance running. Others testify of a closeness they feel toward God while running through open fields. It's good that these folks have found a satisfaction in physical exercise, but *nothing* can take the place of the *person* of Jesus Christ in the life of the believer. One has not been truly "born again'' until he personally receives Christ as Saviour and Lord.

What I'm about to say may seem contradictory after all that has gone before, but the benefits and pleasures of a healthy body gained through running are, after all, only temporal. It is the soul that is eternal. Have we neglected it?

The Apostle Paul said in I Timothy 4:8, "For bodily exercise profiteth little: but godliness is profitable unto all things, having promise of the life that now is, and of that which is to come."

The godliness Paul spoke of is not earned or bought. It is a gift. "For the wages of sin is death; but the gift of God is eternal life through Jesus Christ our Lord"(Romans 6:23). God wants to give you that gift—you receive it by faith—faith in the One who took your place on the cross.

As you close this book and make some decisions about your future jogging and running programs, I hope you'll make some decisions about your future eternity, too.

One day, as you and I stand before God, we may hear Him say, "Ye did run well . . ." (Galatians 5:7a).

Dear Lord

Thank You!